W9-CCD-898

The Information Mosaic

Harvard Business School
Series in Accounting and Control
Series Editor, Robert S. Kaplan

Board of Advisers

Germain B. Boer	Vanderbilt University
Thomas R. Dyckman	Cornell University
Robert K. Elliott	KPMG Peat Marwick
George Foster	Stanford University
Hein Schreuder	University of Limburg

Rewarding Results
  Motivating Profit Center Managers
  by Kenneth A. Merchant

Measures for Manufacturing Excellence
  Edited by Robert S. Kaplan

The Information Mosaic
  by Sharon M. McKinnon and
  William J. Bruns, Jr.

The Information Mosaic

Sharon M. McKinnon
Northeastern University

William J. Bruns, Jr.
Harvard Business School

Foreword by William E. Langdon, Executive Vice President
Society of Management Accountants of Canada

Harvard Business School Press
Boston, Massachusetts

The paper used in this publication meets the requirements of the American National
Standard for Permanence of Paper for the Printed Library Materials Z39.49-1984.

LIBRARY OF CONGRESS CATALOGING-IN-PUBLICATION DATA
McKinnon, Sharon M.
    The information mosaic / Sharon M. McKinnon, William J. Bruns, Jr.
    foreword by William E. Langdon.
        p.   cm.
    Includes bibliographical references and index.
    ISBN 0-87584-317-4 (alk. paper)
    1. Managerial accounting. 2. Management information systems.
  I. Bruns, William J. II. Title.
HF5657.4.M38   1992
    658.4'038—dc20   91-46758
                                                            CIP

Contents

Acknowledgments

DURING the months of research and writing we were fortunate to have the counsel of many friends and colleagues. Without their help the outcome of our project would have been much different.

Special thanks are due the managers who scheduled interviews in each of the twelve companies that took part in the study. Without them we might still be looking for the right managers to interview. Thanks are also due the managers we interviewed. By answering our many questions, they provided the data on which our conclusions are based.

The Society of Management Accountants of Canada and the Division of Research of the Harvard Business School provided generous financial support, which allowed us to build a sample appropriate for the research rather than one based on location and manager availability. We were never asked, "How far are you going?" or "Why did you visit multiple locations or the same location on several trips?" In particular, Alexander Mersereau of the Society and Warren McFarlan of Harvard supported our work enthusiastically, contributed their own ideas to the project, and never reminded us that our original research schedule was overly ambitious. Many colleagues made contributions at different stages of our work. They include: Julie Hertenstein, Robert Kaplan, Kenneth Merchant, Robert Simons, Richard Vancil, and G. Peter Wilson at Harvard; Ronald Copeland, Bairj Donabedian, Mario Maletta, Lynn Marples, Robert Ruland and Arnold Wright at Northeastern; Ramona Dzinkowski and other members of the project review committee—A. S. Williams,

E. C. Cousineau, and G. Wilkinson—at the Society of Management Accountants; and three anonymous reviewers.

As this book neared completion Richard Luecke and Natalie Greenberg of the Harvard Business School Press had many ideas about how the presentation of our data and conclusions could be improved.

Finally, we thank Patricia Powers and the staff of the Word Processing Center of the Harvard Business School. Patty managed the process of turning countless drafts of chapters into a manuscript and finally a book. Without her cheerful help the task would have been more difficult and not nearly as pleasant.

Foreword

THE Society of Management Accountants of Canada (SMAC) is pleased to be involved with the publication of *The Information Mosaic* by Professors Sharon M. McKinnon and William J. Bruns, Jr. This book is a direct result of our call in December 1988 for research on the relevance of management accounting reports and on their impact on managerial decision making. Professors McKinnon and Bruns's work was supported by our research program and by the Division of Research of the Harvard Business School.

The impetus for the project came from our belief that the quality of management decisions is no better than the quality of the accounting and other information upon which they are based. A number of observers have estimated that as many as half of all conventional accounting reports are either not used, or are duplicative in content. There are abundant examples of organizations that do not properly tailor the content and presentation of these reports to user needs.

The absence of relevant management accounting reports seriously inhibits managers from evaluating, formulating, and implementing appropriate courses of action. The Society of Management Accountants of Canada recognizes the important role that certified management accountants (CMAs) must play in improving the quality of management accounting reports.

The Information Mosaic confirms many of these concerns and suspicions about the contribution and shortcomings of conventional management reports and management accounting in manufacturing companies. By revealing the information that managers truly need, and

ix

the sources they actually use to obtain it, this book helps set an agenda for improvements in management accounting and reporting. It challenges management accountants to examine their goals and methods to discover how they can better serve the manager's need for timely, accurate, and relevant information.

Our society is the leading research body in management accounting in Canada, and it contributes significantly to worldwide management accounting research. SMAC is also responsible for the training, accreditation, and continuing professional development of CMAs. We are pleased to have sponsored the research that led to the publication of this important book and extend our appreciation to the participating organizations as well as to the reviewers who provided invaluable input.

William E. Langdon, CMA, FCMA
Executive Vice President

The Information Mosaic

Introduction

"INFORMATION" is certainly the word of the twentieth century. Leaps in information technology capacities have prompted many to term this the Information Age. But have these advances really changed the essence of what managers want to know to do their jobs well? Our research into what information managers use has enabled us to look closely at the reality of management. Our study began as a project to learn about how managers use accounting information, but it evolved to be about more than just information; it is also a study of how managers cope with their management tasks.

Our field study took us into twelve manufacturing companies in Canada and the United States, where we talked with plant managers, sales directors, accountants, and other managers about the information they need to control their daily operations. Early in our interviews, we realized that through our questions about information, we were getting fascinating glimpses into the ingenious ways managers deal with the dynamics of their jobs. Accounting information quickly took its place as only one small piece in a vast mosaic of facts, forecasts, intuition, gossip, and gut feelings competing for the attention of managers.

The impetus for our research came from our common experiences in teaching financial and managerial accounting to executive students. Our exposure to mid- and upper-level managers left us with a sense of discomfort and discontinuity about the role of the material we were teaching and the validity of traditional academic wisdom as to its use in everyday managerial decision making. A casual stroll

1

through the textbook exhibits at academic accounting conventions provides many examples of the beliefs that academics have about the importance of accounting information within the firm. Many textbooks have versions of the following statement in their introductory chapters:

Management processes require information, and accounting is one of the most important information systems within any organization. A thorough understanding of accounting is absolutely necessary if managers are to perform their organizational roles. For this reason, accounting is one of the most important topics for study by future managers. They must learn basic accounting concepts and learn to use accounting information to be able to manage.

Despite the claim that "a thorough understanding of accounting is absolutely necessary," we consistently found that some of the most successful managers in our executive classes had progressed to high levels of responsibility without knowledge of, or exposure to, much of the basic accounting material in introductory textbooks. This naturally led to questions such as: What information *do* managers use in day-to-day operations? Under what circumstances *is* information that we think of as accounting information actually used by managers?

We were also influenced by an earlier accounting research study, *Centralization vs. Decentralization in Organizing the Controller's Department*, by Herbert Simon et al. (1954). This classic field study of organizational controllership noted the existence of "unofficial reports" that showed evidence of constant use—notes, memos, and other informal notations by managers of information they considered vital for their work. Could this still be the case almost forty years later? The explosion of information technology would seem to have produced such an advanced state of choices that MBLN—"management by little notebook"—should be absurd. Yet it was intriguing to us to consider that this might still be the case. Throughout our interviews, we kept an eye out for the existence of the little notebook with all the vital facts kept handy in the left-hand drawer. Later chapters of this text detail evidence that managers continue to rely on this type of information.

The question of what information managers actually use seems like a basic research issue that should have been explored in great detail during the forty years since the Simon study. Yet in our search for literature to build on and to guide us, we found little that addresses the content of managerial information needs. Scholars in industrial and social psychology, organizational behavior, management, accounting, and systems development have addressed issues of human decision making, characteristics of managerial work habits, sources of managerial information, and theories of information use patterns.

Norman Macintosh (1985) provided the best recent summary of this work, summarizing succinctly where we stand at the present time:

Although the cumulative results of studies of this kind have been inconclusive and inconsistent, the long run potential for tailoring our systems to the unique characteristics of the individual manager remains tantalizing. (p. 7)

He later concluded optimistically:

The general idea of matching individual differences to information system characteristics seems highly practical and well within the group of designers. In its simplest form it is merely a systematic way of carrying out user needs assessments. . . . (p. 108)

The studies that support these conclusions provide a context in which to understand issues of information content, and we refer to many of them throughout the body of this study.

Simon (1954) and Robert Anthony (1965) laid some theoretical groundwork for study of information content, but in recent history there has been little accounting research in this area. Robert Simons (1991) presented one of the few recent frameworks for analyzing these issues. We will discuss these three authors briefly in the next section. Although accounting information is only a small part of the information used by most managers, much research by accounting academics has assumed that such information is the most relevant or the only information managers use. Furthermore, the focus of much of this research has been to explore the correlation between exposure to a piece of accounting information and the existence of a specific decision afterward. Yet the fact that a decision was made after information was received is not proof that the decision was influenced by that particular information.

James March (1987, p. 40) also summarized the status of our knowledge very succinctly: ". . . careful information about the ways in which decision makers use information and make decisions is scarce. There are remarkably few analyses of what managers actually

do with their time, or what information they use or might use."
March concluded that without such knowledge, it is difficult or impossible to adapt systems to observed characteristics of human beings.
Yet changing the ways humans make decisions or replacing them with
machines seem to be elusive objectives at the present time.

Relevant Terminology

Although our focus in this book is not on accounting information as anything more than one piece in the information mosaic,
we did begin our research as accountants seeking to understand the
use of our own subject matter. Given that this initial focus shaped
many of the questions we asked, it is probably useful to define exactly
(or inexactly) what accounting information is considered to be.

The boundary between accounting information and other information used by managers is not easy to delineate. The Committee on
the Foundations of Accounting Measurement grappled with where to
place such a boundary (American Accounting Association, 1971). It
concluded "that neither accounting nor a management information
system is a subset of the other," but that "does not mean that processing and analysis of nonfinancial data should be permanently ex-
cluded from the field of accounting." (p. 11) Its broad definition of
accounting measurement helps clarify the boundary: "Accounting
measurement is an assignment of numerals to an entity's past, present,
or future economic phenomena, on the basis of observation and according to rules." (p. 3)

Accounting information is quantitative, relates to an entity, is
based on observation, and is prepared according to rules. Data and
information that do not meet these tests are not accounting information but may be used by managers and may be important in a management information system.

The same committee dwelt at length on the distinction between
a primary measure—a number generated directly by quantifying the
property of an object—and a secondary measure—a number that is
derived indirectly by an algebraic transformation of a set of numbers
that are direct measures of some objects or their attributes. Primary
measures include counts of inflows, outflows, and balances on nonmonetary goods; physical quantities; prices for nonmonetary goods;
and counts of inflows, outflows, and balances of monetary goods and
obligations. Using this distinction, a cash balance is a "primary mea-

sure" based on a "count," while information on income is a "secondary measure." The committee noted that "only a few primary measures are used in accounting, since even in the counting process some algebraic transformation is often involved."

These distinctions in characteristics of information had been noted earlier by Simon et al. (1954):

In those companies where the products can be measured, at least roughly, in physical units, manufacturing and some sales executives make more use of data expressed in physical units than data expressed in dollars . . . . In most companies there was a relatively high relationship between the receptivity of operating personnel to accounting data and the willingness of the accounting department to report data in physical units or to relate them to physical units. (p. 3)

Simon also addressed how accounting data can be used by managers in a now well-known classification: (1) as a score-card for overall appraisal of an operating unit, (2) to direct attention to problems that need to be solved, and (3) to aid in the solution of problems. He stated that

the significance of reports lies in reminding executives of things they already know and placing these things in proper quantitative perspective, rather than hinting to them things they never suspected and are unable to trace down to their causes. (p. 22)

Anthony (1965) also addressed characteristics of information used by managers in his development of a classification scheme for dealing with planning and control systems. His three categories of managerial activity are (1) strategic planning, (2) management control, and (3) operational control. Strategic planning is future-oriented and involves nonrepetitive, creative decision making by high-level individuals. Management control is involved with maintaining effective and efficient performance and is characterized by interpersonal interactions. Operational control assures daily tasks are carried out effectively. The types of information needed for these activities would differ. For example, strategic planning might use unstructured, future-oriented, externally derived information, while operational control might use daily or weekly status reports.

For analyzing management control systems, Simons (1991) has developed a new framework that recognizes the types of systems in which managers should find accounting systems most useful. Boundary systems determine the limits of acceptable action and activities within organizations. Interactive systems are created by top managers to focus attention on what is important to them and to influence strategic direction and control. Accounting information and accounting systems may be used interactively, but so can other kinds of systems. But diagnostic systems are created by organizations to provide feedback on processes and performance so managers can monitor activities and fine-tune operations. Accounting information is often important in systems that are used diagnostically, and many accounting reports and systems are intended to be diagnostic systems or to support such systems.

The Relationship between Accounting and Information Systems

Almost every organization of any size has managers whose primary responsibilities include serving information needs of other managers. A major function of an accounting or a controller's department is to collect, process, and disseminate information to managers. These management accounting systems are frequently what come to mind when the question of where managers get information is raised. The systems developed and managed by accounting professionals are comprehensive, systematic, reliable, and unbiased in most organizations. They support other accounting responsibilities such as reporting to investors, and tax and regulatory authorities. But there are important reasons why accounting systems can never be sufficient in meeting managers' needs for information.

Accountants collect data by directly observing activities or by examining, collecting, and processing documents created by those who directly observe or cause events and activities to take place. Using these data, management accountants measure the effects of transactions, events, and activities, and classify, aggregate, allocate, and summarize those measurements into accounting reports. Reports can be comprehensive, representing the activities and results of operations of the entire organization, or they can be specialized for a particular function or manager. The reports publicize the information and make it readily available and easy to store.

In the past, the ability of an accounting system to provide information for managers was frequently limited by difficulties in collection and summary and the limitations of manual and paper-based processing. With electronic data processing, data today can be stored, manipulated, and transmitted from one place to another and instantly accessed throughout an organization. Accounting departments were the first to utilize modern data processing equipment in many companies, and some are still the primary managers of information systems. In other companies, however, the electronic data processing functions have been separated from the accounting function, and an information services function or management information system (MIS) stands ready to serve all managers, including those in the accounting department. Whether the accounting function and the data and information function are separate or combined, they are often thought to be the primary sources of information available to managers in an organization.

Most organizations expend considerable resources trying to tailor their internal management accounting and reporting systems to the needs of management at various levels. It is not unusual to find careful attention given to information requests and to comments and criticism of regular reports. Managers in most organizations describe much of this information as indispensable. However, these same managers make it clear that existing accounting and information systems are not sufficient to meet their needs. As a result, every manager creates and uses a personal information system, which is supported by direct observation and interpersonal contacts within and outside the company.

Managers' needs to supplement formal information systems have been noted in many research studies. Henry Mintzberg (1973) and John Kotter (1982) described the apparent restlessness of managers who move from place to place observing activity and talking with people. In their popular book, *In Search of Excellence*, Thomas Peters and Robert Waterman (1982) glorified MBWA—"management by walking around," and they concluded it is essential to informal communication in excellent companies. These activities are very much a part of the personal information systems used by managers in every organization. When the size of a company facility or geographic separation makes this form of informative communication impossible, managers try to accomplish the same thing by telephone, electronic mail, and facsimile communications. The need for information to carry out their missions drives managers to seek it directly—even before it can be processed by the organization's formal information channels.

The kind of data collected by managers as they move about their facilities observing and talking to others has a very different character from the information provided by an accounting or information system. Data are collected in a more elemental form. Quantities, which will be converted to monetary measurements in the accounting process, are observed physically or counted. Idle employees observed on a production line have a different impact on a manager than a dollar measure of the cost of idle time. A warehouse so full that it can receive no more finished product demands a manager's attention much more quickly than a report on resources invested in inventory. The observations are concrete; the reports are abstractions. These activities might not be thought of as part of the information systems in a company at first glance, but they do provide information that is highly valued by managers. Accountants and information systems managers can learn much about improving formal information systems by observing the way managers collect and use information from their personal systems.

Research Questions

We designed our research study to focus on four related sets of issues:

What information do managers say they need and use? We expected managers to describe their information needs and use in relation to the tasks and activities they see as their work. We were interested in their sources of information, the form in which information was received, and the frequency of updating. We expected that there would be differences between information used on a daily or frequent basis and information used less frequently. We expected managers to be sensitive to the timeliness and perceived reliability of information. We were also interested in the metric and degree of aggregation managers seek in the information they use. Finally, we expected to find differences in the kind of information managers use based on their level in organizational hierarchies and the time period relevant to their tasks and activities.

Where do managers get the information they use? Are management accounting and management information systems serving managers well? If not, why not? Previous studies show that managers place great reliance on personal information systems. We wanted to learn why managers develop and use personal information systems and whether those systems are redundant to accounting and management information systems or whether they have been developed because corporate systems fail to meet their needs. Implicit in these issues is the question of whether the design of a management accounting or management information system can be used to enhance the usefulness of information for managers and thus the managers' effectiveness. Have some companies been able to develop more effective systems than others? And if so, what are the characteristics of those systems?

Are some managers better prepared to use information than others? Management background and training are usually major factors in personnel selection and promotion schemes. Information is important, and some managers may be able to use information more effectively than others. Perhaps that should be a factor in management selection and promotion schemes. Can training help managers learn to use information more effectively? We were interested in the possibility that information systems could be matched to background or function if functional managers cited the need for information with similar characteristics or similar time horizons.

How has the development of the personal computer and MIS and data communication technology affected the ways in which managers obtain and use information? The most frequent justification for acquiring data processing and communication equipment is that it will improve the quality of information available to managers. We hoped managers would be able to tell us if, in their view, this has been the case. The popular business press has promulgated the view that computers are on the verge of revolutionizing how managers get information. Are the computers and terminals in executive offices being used and if so, how? Have managers or their companies been able to analyze or measure improvements in information efficiency or availability?

How We Chose to Study These Questions

There are numerous routes through which questions about managerial behavior can be studied, all of which have been taken by researchers in the past. A common methodology is the observation of manager behavior to collect data. For a sample of reasonable size, observation of manager behavior requires large amounts of time from both managers and observers. Necessarily, the observation process is intrusive and, except where managers' activities are fairly routine, the behavior observed is determined in part by the unique circumstances during the period observation takes place.

Another way to study information use by managers is to ask

them what they use. Using this method obviously implies that the researcher believes that the answers will be honest representations of reality. We decided to employ this latter method through a large field study during which we visited managers in their offices. The trust necessary to validate findings from this type of methodology came quickly. We found that most managers are excited about what they do. They know what they need to do their jobs well; they know if they are getting what they need, and they are vocal if they are not.

Before we could begin this study, we had to decide exactly what to ask managers and how to get them to participate in our study. We conducted a pilot study with a mail questionnaire to get a glimpse of what types of information managers used. A description of the pilot study and some results are included in Appendix III. Although they are not the basis for conclusions drawn from the major field study, the results are not inconsistent with conclusions drawn from the field study.

During the field study itself we conducted interviews with seventy-three managers in twelve manufacturing corporations in North America, six each in the United States and Canada. The Society of Management Accountants of Canada co-sponsored the research with the Division of Research of the Harvard Business School and played a major role in contacting Canadian businesses and in ensuring the ultimate success of the project. The corporations taking part in our study were a nonrandom sample selected on the basis of location and accessibility, personal contacts, and expected willingness to help with the research process. When possible, companies with similarities to those already selected for study were contacted in hopes of keeping some control on organizational diversity. All companies surveyed were engaged in manufacturing, marketing, and distribution, and each was a member of one of three groups: heavy manufacturing of basic materials and products, high-tech manufacturing, and consumer branded product manufacturing. All but three were large organizations and all had significant presence in their respective industries. Exhibit I-1 gives a brief description and summarizes some of the characteristics of the companies that took part in this study. Company names have been disguised.

We asked our contact in each firm to identify at least five managers who would be willing to spend an hour answering our questions. We asked for a minimum of two managers each in production and sales or marketing functions, and at least one manager involved in information provision such as accounting or information systems. We specified that we wanted senior-level managers if possible. When the managers were identified, we sent each a letter stating that we were going to focus on what information they use in their jobs. Exhibit I-2 lists the managers interviewed by job title, revealing that most had major responsibilities for sales and marketing, production and manu-facturing, or staff functions. Their functions and tenure both with the company and in their present jobs confirmed that they were expe-rienced managers. We made no attempt to determine if they were effective managers, though most had been promoted to their current responsibilities after several years of experience with their company.

Our next task was to design an interview questionnaire, or proto-col, to guide our questions. We chose to focus questions about infor-mation around the activities in which managers engage, and thus the interviews began with a request for the manager to describe at least three activities typical of his or her responsibilities. The interview protocol is presented in Appendix II. In addition to questions about activities and information, it includes sections on useful reports, office communications, performance evaluation, computer use, and demo-graphics.

Over a period of eight months, we traveled from one coast to another, as far north as Bracebridge, Ontario and as far south as the Carolinas. A typical day would have us arrive at the company early in the morning for a briefing with our contact, who was frequently the controller or the plant manager. We would then split up with our tape recorders and questionnaires and head to the offices of our interviewees. Our visits often included lunch with other managers, during which we gained informal insights about their positions, and we usually were able to wrangle a plant tour at the end of the day.

Many people have asked how we were able to get busy managers to agree to spend an hour or more answering questions, and we wor-ried about this ourselves in designing our study. What we found was that even those managers who seemed to be slotting us into very crowded schedules relaxed and opened up within minutes. People love to talk about what they do, and more often than not the hour flew by. Our managers also were not reticent about speaking with a tape recorder going, even when they were criticizing their company's policies or expressing frustration. We left the interviews confident that these managers had been candid and insightful with us. They made this project truly an enjoyable experience, and one from which we have learned a great deal not only about information use, but also about the individual roles people play in business organizations.

Exhibit I-1 Participants in the Research (names have been disguised)

Companies (listed in order of size)	General Description	Comments	Number of Managers Interviewed
Worldwide Computer Co., Inc.	Manufactures, sells, and services computer and systems hardware and software to diversified industry markets.	Well known for distinctive management style and systems. Currently restructuring major functions.	5
Canadian Oil & Gas, Ltd.	Large producer, refiner, and marketer of petroleum materials and products.	Integrated operations from field to retail sales locations.	6
Belton Foods Co., Inc.	Manufactures and distributes branded consumer food products throughout the world.	Strong brands and high volume sales in United States dominate competitors in several product lines.	10
Dell Chemicals, Ltd.	Large producer and distributor of industrial chemicals, coatings, and explosives.	Integrated producer for both external sales and downstream products.	8
Stanga Steel, Ltd.	Large iron and steel manufacturer serving construction and manufacturing industries in both United States and Canada.	Manufacturing and sales of both specialty and commodity steel products.	6

the company computing resources. The personal attitudes of our non-user managers can be summarized by the following four actual statements which are typical of what nonusers in our study told us.

1. "Computers make managers do things their subordinates should be doing."
2. "Personal relationships are the key to doing my job well."
3. "The computer doesn't add anything to the hard-copy report."
4. "I used to use it a lot, but now I'm waiting for something more useful, like artificial intelligence."

The first statement was repeated by younger and older nonusers alike in firms whose computer environments ranged from dark ages to state of the art. Respondents who seemed most uncomfortable with their admission of nonuse fell back on this defensive, but probably truthful, response. This issue arose frequently from our open-ended question concerning how computerization had affected a manager's ability to manage personally. A common response was the ability to reduce the number of people in a particular function with the advent of computerization. Indeed, present cost reduction programs in many companies in both the United States and Canada are eliminating layers of middle management, and personal computer use by upper management levels may be part of why this can occur. Managers may be reluctant to change the boundaries they believe define their executive position, either from fear of losing power or from a genuine belief that their time is better spent doing other things.

The second statement reflects many managers' belief that computer communication fails to convey the nuances of personal communication; that the personalities and relationships between individuals are more important than any benefits they associate with computerization. A sales manager noted that his field sales staff could very easily send their reports through a terminal or a facsimile transmission, but that instead they call in weekly. These weekly calls enable them to catch up on office stories and maintain a sort of umbilical cord to him and the organization.

The third statement points out that computerization of information in itself frequently fails to enhance other channels. Zuboff (1988) noted that workers switching from a paper to an on-line system frequently experience the inclination to revert to the old papers, which have a physical, sensory, touchable nature on which extra notes can be written. Their source is known, whereas information on screens seems to appear out of nowhere and to go to an unknown place. Similarly, our managers often remarked about the need to have a piece of paper to jot notes on, or a printout to carry on an airplane to read.

I find it tough to sit in front of a terminal reading numbers or mail. I like to have it on a piece of paper that I can stick in my briefcase, take home with me, and jot notes in the margin. I don't find it useful to be tied to a machine.

If the information available on a computer screen is also on a written report, the managers we interviewed tend to prefer the latter every time. The major advantage of a terminal is the timeliness of the data it supplies, but even real-time systems have problems. First, real-time systems still must frequently have data input by human operators. Humans may be behind in their data input; thus a supposed real-time screen has information items in differing stages of being up-to-date. Second, real-time has no meaning for much data, particularly financial data. A manager interested in following divisional earnings states that Tuesday's depreciation charges, utility costs, overhead, and so forth, mean nothing to him, even though he can tune in daily to check earnings. Earnings begin to seem meaningful only on a monthly basis. The monthly report that lands on his desk within a few days serves his real-time data needs sufficiently. Third, much of a manager's information needs may be met from external sources. While checking the company's stock quote may be interesting to a manager, newspapers and trade journals fill this need plus many others that even an external data service fails to enhance.

The fourth statement ("I used to use it . . . now I'm waiting for something . . . .") characterizes a type of manager whose actions go contrary to the general belief (Rockart and Treacy, 1982, for example) that once a manager begins using a personal computer he is hooked for life. Several of our managers indicated that they had used computers much more extensively in the past than now. In essence, the charm and the fun had worn off as they realized that they were spending more and more time at a terminal without commensurate benefits. A senior marketing manager at Worldwide Computer explained how he had come to hold this view:

Senior managers don't have time to sit in front of a computer. I've been through that stage as a staff person. I used to sit in front of that thing all the time and it would save me a day a week. Then it started to cost me a day a week.

Many managers in this group tended to be relatively young and many had technical backgrounds. They were not afraid of the technology, but were simply waiting for some future application such as artificial intelligence or an executive information system (EIS) that would justify resuming their personal use.

The Absence of DSS and EIS

Part of the problems experienced by the managers in our study may be the absence of specialized information systems designed for their needs. The past several years have generated considerable interest in decision support systems (DSS) or executive information systems designed to provide the upper-level manager or executive with an array of information, both internal and external, needed for managerial decision making. Popular business publications have noted the development of several systems and indicated that their effectiveness in experimental stages appears to be justifying their costs. The general impression left with the reader is that these systems will be ubiquitous within several years and that the company without one will be left in the dust.

This may be the case, but the companies in our study provide good examples of the difficulties inherent in development of these systems. The controller of one of the most technologically advanced companies in our study, a leader in hardware development, admitted that his company's greatest void was in providing management information systems for executives. Managers expressed the need for such diverse types of information from such different sources that effective systems would almost have to be designed individually, as plant manager Ben Scott designed the system described earlier in this chapter. Another challenge to implementation of decision support systems is the nonroutine, frequently external nature of much of the information used by managers in high positions. Finally, sometimes top-level managers are unable to tell staff or subordinates what they need because they want to maintain confidentiality. As one senior manager told us: "I use my PC primarily for analysis, especially for analyses where confidentiality is required . . . possible acquisitions, for example." In such situations, high-level managers will continue to be on their own.

Retrieval of information from different sources may be the biggest stumbling block for most of the companies in our study and, we suspect, for many others as well. Executives who want to compare sales orders, present warehouse availability, and long-term production schedules in order to make operating or strategic decisions could need to combine data that would come from at least three different databases in the company. Data compatibility poses major problems beyond merely anticipating the desired relationships when programming the systems. What appear to be simple comparisons can become nightmares when data specifications are different from function to function. An example is found at Cancoil, where different formats for customer addresses in the sales and delivery databases prevented effective merging of the two.

One of our companies, Communications Equipment, has an executive information system in the works. The corporate controller, who uses his personal computer daily and wishes other managers did as well, pointed out to us that the new system will have two "advantages" that should lead to its success. First, printing from the system will be blocked, necessitating looking at the screen for data; and second, secretaries will not have access to any of the information screens, thus ensuring personal use by executives. On the other hand, we wonder what will happen when this system is offered to managers who think like the nonusers we discussed in the previous section of this chapter.

Electronic Communication

Our interviews provided a vivid picture of the uses of electronic media in communication and as means by which information is obtained by managers. In particular, managers told us how they use electronic mail, voice mail, and facsimile machines. For most managers, these are less-preferred alternatives to face-to-face communications or telephone, except in certain situations. But they cover distances more quickly than letter mail or memoranda, and their timeliness is valued.

All but two of our companies had some form of E-mail in use to some degree. One large global company has a system that is used heavily by everyone to the extent that many managers receive hundreds of messages per day. Of the five managers interviewed from this company, only one indicated that the electronic mail situation produced information overload. The remaining four believed that the system enabled them to keep track of extraordinary amounts of company data. When we asked one manager how he could deal with seventy or eighty E-mail messages each day, he told us:

I deal with it through a very good secretary. She goes through it and categorizes the mail. I get a folder from her at the beginning and end of the day, and it's prioritized . . . priority items, reports . . . half dozen categories. It's printed out.

He could have been speaking for his four colleagues because each of them had a similar procedure for having a secretary print messages out on hard copy, frequently screening and categorizing them as well. We encountered the same procedure in other companies. This would seem to negate the proposed immediacy value of electronic mail, turning it into simply another, albeit faster and more reliable, company mail system.

The primary advantage we encountered in the use of electronic mail was the ability to communicate instantly with foreign operating units. Within one company location, electronic mail was often used, but its use seemed to be only an extension of the telephone, often being sent only as a written reminder of oral communication. However, with the geographic dispersion of operations, the use of electronic mail assumed major significance as a means of instant communications through numerous time zones. One manager told us:

For communicating with my counterparts in Singapore, the Netherlands, and Japan, E-mail is the best form of communication because I don't have to remember what time it is.

Another would agree:

Computerization has certainly simplified the control of a worldwide sales force. I can send a message to all six regions and get an answer back from every one of them in 24 hours. I couldn't possibly do that on the telephone.

One interesting side note is that many managers who use electronic mail claim mainly to receive rather than to initiate messages. This actually makes sense when you consider how often one message is sent to many recipients, with little incremental effort required as more recipients are added to the address list.

From a behavioral standpoint, electronic mail lets management levels communicate without going through the normal reporting hierarchy. This has its good and bad consequences. One manager speculated that his boss must get hundreds of messages daily from people trying to impress him by how hard they are working. When the superior in question was interviewed later in the day, he admitted that might be the case. Nevertheless, he claimed that he thrived on overload, that his major ability as a manager was the ability to scan vast quantities of data and choose the one item that was most valuable.

An electronic mail message may also seem to need a response when none is really required, thus causing unnecessary reaction and more messages. An electronically printed message may be imbued with a certain amount of concrete legitimacy that invokes the sense of a needed response more than some other form of communication. And when the boss notes "looks good" on a message about a proposal, the ramifications of its instant communication throughout the company may have impact beyond what an offhand oral comment might have had.

Because of the varying nature of the electronic mail systems in the companies we visited, few comparisons can be made. However, we did note some generalities. First, executives do use electronic mail, but they seem to be quick to qualify their use as minimal personally. Many expressed that personal interaction with peers and others was their major form of communication because of the intangible perceptions that are screened out by a terminal. They also are contemptuous of managers who use electronic mail to avoid personal confrontation. Second, electronic mail is frequently used as a way to create a tangible record of a personal communication. "I'll send you an E-mail message to confirm these details," is a common example of this use. This is an interesting use in that it uses the tool for a purpose that the tool may be intended to avoid—that is, the need for a printed medium. Third, many use electronic mail like a telephone answering machine, to ensure that a message has reached another party when that party is not available for a personal conversation. Whether this use (or the telephone answering machine) defines a true advantage over a simple letter is a function of time. It depends on how frequently the receiver or the receiver's surrogate checks messages versus how fast a physical mail system could deliver the same message. Time of delivery, personal contact, and knowledge of receipt were captured in one thought by the corporate controller at Engineering Software when he told us:

E-mail is well used in our international operations. But here it's not so useful. Personal contact is so easy. And you know it gets personal attention. If I send an E-mail message to my superior, I don't know whether he will read it today or tomorrow or a week later. But if I walk to his office and push my head in, I know I have his attention and that he will get the message.

Fourth, individuals who do not use a personal computer for other uses are the least likely to use electronic mail personally. They may feel compelled to participate in this communication medium, particularly if the company atmosphere encourages its use, but they avoid personal participation by enlisting the aid of secretaries or subordinates.

While we expected to encounter significant use of electronic mail, we were unprepared for the extent to which facsimile use has spread in the few years since its introduction. Many of the same advantages and disadvantages surrounding electronic mail are applicable to the FAX machine, but there are important differences. The only disadvantages we noted for FAX use were that its expense is greater than that for electronic mail and that outside parties can clutter receivers with junk FAX. These disadvantages seem to be more than offset by several other factors. First, anyone with a telephone can use a FAX machine without much instruction and without significant capital outlay. Therefore most business entities can receive messages, and a message may be sent without the need to turn on a computer and type one's way through the mail system. Second, a message may consist of or contain varying content, including handwritten notes, drawings, maps, and so forth, that convey more of a detailed or personal communication than a typewritten message.

Some uses of the FAX we encountered involved communications with foreign business entities. Stanga Steel's maintenance foreman noted that communications with the German builder of Stanga's new computerized furnace are all by FAX. Messages and diagrams go back and forth daily as the bugs are worked out of the system. An English-speaking sales manager at Cancoil believes that the FAX helps him communicate with his French-speaking colleagues more easily. Each has a certain limited proficiency in the other's language, but the visual nature of a FAX message allows time for each to understand the other more fully. An electronic mail message might seem to do the same, but this manager claims that it is too impersonal for his tastes.

The final entrant in the new electronic communication is voice mail. By extending the capability of the telephone to receive and store messages if the intended recipient is busy, away from the telephone, or already using the telephone, voice mail permits the timely exchange of information in situations where an ordinary telephone system would fail. Furthermore, as in the case of E-mail, the same message can be addressed to many telephone mailboxes at the same time. And, as with E-mail, time differences between the sending and receiving points can be ignored. These advantages, along with the richness of verbal communication with its ability to capture voice inflection and intensity, portend the likely spread and early acceptance of voice-mail systems by managers.

In summary, electronic mail, FAX, and voice-mail systems are seen as useful tools by the managers in our study, and their use is growing. Electronic mail has certain disadvantages in its impersonality, but it does seem to increase the channels of communication between levels in organizations. The FAX is seen as more personable and easier to use, and these benefits appear to offset its relatively higher cost. In many situations, the biggest threat to greater use of E-mail systems will come from the combination of FAX and voice mail, both of which are seen by managers as easier to use and friendlier media.

Summary

The twelve companies in our study are not necessarily typical of American or Canadian companies in general, but they do have many of the same characteristics as other companies. All have been prosperous financially to differing degrees; each has taken steps to improve its management information systems, although some are not as far along as others in the process; and each has achieved a certain level of computerization in its manufacturing processes. We believe that their managers have enough in common with managers in most manufacturing companies that our observations about them can be generalized to a larger population of U.S. and Canadian firms.

The patterns of use we observed support a conclusion that information systems and personal computers have been put in place because technology has allowed them to be, rather than because of needs or consideration of the value of technology to enhance connections or relationships. As a result, not all managers have embraced the new technology and learned to use it effectively. Some who have tried to use the new technology have given up because other methods of getting information have a higher value-to-effort ratio in their jobs or experience. Those managers who have mastered information system technology supplied by the company or tailored part of a system to provide for personal needs use it more, and many depend on these new tools.

Electronic mail is a major use of personal computers and information systems in many companies, but it does not necessarily lead to greater use of personal computers for other types of work. Obstacles to extended use cited by managers were primarily a belief that more personal contacts with others were more effective, and incompatible database arrangements that make it difficult to get needed data together in a way that it can easily be used. The number of managers who reported entering data from hard copy reports into their own system's spreadsheet or analysis program may be a harbinger of greater computer use in the future as more compatible systems and databases bridge the incompatibility problems that discourage many managers from greater use.

Use of personal computers was greatest in those cases where managers had some control over the design of their system or had specific uses necessitated by their positions. The absence of procedures for justifying equipment or software purchases or the means to measure whether equipment is used effectively has put equipment in the hands of managers who do not need it and see no present use for it, but who want to be ready to use it when it will finally serve them. In the meantime, they use other means of getting the information they need to manage. The personal computer revolution has not really started yet in many offices, even though the weapons are available and often sitting on desks or office credenzas. As Michael Schrage (1990) noted, in general, organizations acquire information technology like Imelda Marcos acquired shoes, without knowing what they are trying to accomplish. Those managers who have figured out what they want to do and have been given the control to develop applications to meet their needs give us the best examples of how computer and system resources can be utilized more effectively.

PART **III**

Making Information More Valuable
to Managers

MANAGERS value information that they trust and can use in their work. Personal observation and management work itself are two of the most important sources of the information managers value and use. Other people are a third important source of information to managers, especially when they have established themselves as reliable providers of information. Reports prepared by others are frequently sources of information, whether they are informal or are provided as outputs of a management accounting or information system.

To have value to a manager, information must be timely, accurate, and relevant. Although these characteristics are similar to the fundamental criteria on which all accounting is based, accounting systems do not provide the information managers value most. Accounting takes time, and other sources of information can satisfy managers' information needs more quickly. Accounting information is financial in nature, and managers act and decide on the basis of physical quantities. Information from management accounting systems is of greatest value in corroborating the impressions about organizational performance and reinforcing prior understanding of the links between actions and results. Accounting information is of greatest value to managers as they contemplate their effectiveness and the success of their decisions and strategies.

None of the managers interviewed complained of information overload. We concluded that managers try to use any information they can find. The nearest thing to a problem with overload occurs

193

when information arrives poorly organized or on too many pieces of paper with an inadequate summary of highlights.

Management accountants who are willing to learn about the true information needs of the managers they serve and to employ new methods to meet those needs can contribute much to the success of their companies. Providing day-to-day operating data to managers in physical terms may be as easy as installing meters, collecting data in different ways, or appointing human monitors who can report. Reports can be customized to match managers' needs, training, and experience.

Available technology should be part of the solutions to serving managers' information needs. But technology alone will not guarantee better information for managers. Only when systems are designed with each manager's needs and preferences in mind will every manager be well served by management accounting and the information mosaic be complete and effective.

What Gives Information Value
to Managers

AS managers described the information they use, we were able to discern much about the characteristics of information that they find of value. Our findings suggest that accountants and information system managers can do much to improve the ways in which their reports and systems provide data and information. Effective information systems cannot exist in isolation from the managers they serve; in many cases, managers are important parts of the systems that satisfy their information needs.

Sources of Valuable
Management Information

Observation is the source of much information that managers find valuable. Managers believe what they see, and they use information that they gather in the process of overseeing the physical manifestations of their work. Manufacturing managers observe processes, interruptions, work pace, and output. Sales and marketing managers observe orders and order processing, shipments, shipping documents, and the mood and work pace of associates. The idea that managers must be supplied with a steady flow of formalized information in order to track the status of their activities was true for none of the managers we interviewed. We have already reported the recognized importance and value of managing by walking around. Managers are continually updating the set of personal, informally

195

sourced information they use in making judgments and managing their responsibilities.

The work that managers do creates information as well. Work orders, directions, approvals, and meetings with superiors and subordinates all result in things happening, and managers observe and remember those things. A logistics manager who has just approved loading a truck with a shipment for an important customer knows that the truck is no longer available until sufficient time has passed that it can return to the transportation pool. Any attempt to design an information system as efficient as the observation and memory of every manager is likely to fail the test of timeliness.

A third source that gives information value to managers is other people. When managers meet to receive reports or to make inquiries of one another, they choose people who they believe will be reliable information providers. Telephone inquiries are included in this source. If information is needed for action or review, a telephone call to another manager who can observe the situation directly or who has already obtained the needed information is an effective way for a manager to get up-to-date information that will be of immediate value.

Managers develop knowledge and relationships that enable them to anticipate where valued information can be found when the need for it is recognized. If a type of information is needed only sporadically, the manager will rely on his or her memory of where similar information was obtained the last time it was needed. Since the reliability of information from that source was established previously, any response to a new inquiry will be seen as equally reliable and valuable.

Informal repetitive reports are a fourth source of valuable information. The recurring need for the same kind of information often leads to a formalization of an information-gathering process and regular provision of familiar categories of information. In a previous chapter, we noted that the plant manager at Belton Foods asks each shift foreman to report total downtime at the end of each shift. A sales or marketing manager may establish a procedure whereby he or she receives information daily about orders scheduled for shipment but not actually shipped. The value of this information is high in spite of its short-term relevance. The source is known, and the reliability of the information is easily assessed.

Telephone, facsimile, and electronic mail systems allow rapid transfer of information from a known observer to a manager who wants the information. The origin and source of the information are known, and further inquiry for clarification is easy. Managers believe that information received by facsimile (and to a lesser extent, information received by electronic mail) is valuable and they seem confident about acting on it.

Finally, there is a high value associated with well-designed periodic reports from an accounting or management information system. Regular reports from information providers are cited as the most useful information for assessing whether long-term goals and objectives have been achieved. They reinforce the relationships between the short-term information managers use on a day-to-day basis and the long-term performance of the manager or operating unit.

Periodic reports, especially accounting reports, serve another function in the information process. In files or notebooks they become the locus of memory that managers use to associate current conditions and possible action with outcomes from similar situations in the past. A decline in orders or reference to the effect on profitability caused by a change in the level of production reinforces a manager's understanding of the implications and importance of recurring events. Eventually these associations may be incorporated in the mental model that a manager uses to guide day-to-day judgments, decisions, and actions.

Characteristics of Valuable Management Information

Three characteristics are required to make information useful: timeliness, accuracy, and relevance. Every person, whether a manager or not, uses these same criteria in assessing whether news reports, consumer information, or weather forecasts should be used as the basis for personal choices and actions. What may be a surprise is the degree to which, in their attempts to obtain information that meet these criteria, managers have constructed their own networks to supplement those created by management accountants and information specialists. A major function of many of these self-constructed personal networks is to corroborate the information received from formal information sources. To a point, redundancy in the information received by managers enhances the value of available information and increases confidence that the information is accurate.

Timeliness, accuracy, and relevance are fundamental criteria addressed by the Financial Accounting Standards Board in its conceptual framework for financial accounting and reporting project (Financial Accounting Standards Board, 1984). Its criterion of relevance incorporates the requirement for timeliness. Its criterion of reliability incorporates the requirement that "information about an item must be representationally faithful, verifiable, and neutral . . . sufficiently free of error and bias . . ." (paragraph 75, p. 26) Therefore it would appear that if the corporate accounting function is performing to its own industry standards, its output would be useful to operating managers. However, this usually was not the case in the companies we studied.

What is wrong with accounting data? First, much accounting data are considered "old news" by the time they are reported to operating managers. Accounting recognition and measurement criteria delay recognition of events until uncertainties have been resolved. Second, accounting information is frequently organized and presented in forms that limit its usefulness to operating managers. Most accounting information is financial in nature, and our conclusions are that physical quantity data are most relevant for everyday operations. Decisions and actions are based on physical quantities, not financial attributes. The manner in which accountants apply their fundamental recognition criteria limits the usefulness of accounting information for day-to-day management, and we want to address some of these problems further.

Timeliness

Much of the information generated by accounting is spurred by transactions that flow from an accounting transaction process such as material requisitions, payroll, order booking, or billing. Yet operating managers are most interested in current information about physical flows. Usually by the time data on downtime, output, labor hours, orders, and so forth have made their way through a reporting system, too much time has elapsed for the information to be actionable. Computerization could possibly fix some of these problems, but this seems not to have been the case to date. The managers we interviewed frequently cited some piece of data that they would like to have on a real-time basis but were unable to get efficiently. One manager told us that production line downtime as it occurred each day is the one piece of information that would prove helpful but that he does not receive. Consider the problem inherent in this request. When a machine breaks down, a cue is needed to report the malfunction to a system. When the cue must be generated from an individual (as opposed to electronically within a machine), it requires action that is nonroutine and may be difficult to program into a job description. Even assuming that the cue is entered into a system immediately, the manager still must be alerted to the existence of the cue. Most operations managers spend little time glued to a computer terminal and thus would miss much of the real-time information value of the cue.

Another manager wanted real-time quality control data. As with downtime statistics, these data are sporadic physical unit data not connected to an accounting transaction process. By the time accounting has compiled the data and transformed them into measurements and reports, their operational value has been diminished. One production manager told us that even a printed record of process control was unnecessary:

We had terminals in the . . . plant installed all over the floor so workers could check how processes were going. They decided they wanted a printer. I pulled it out the next day. That information has time value that is instant with the process. Provided that information helps maintain the process, then they don't need a record that they have in fact maintained it.

A third manager acknowledged the importance of cost data from accounting, even citing the monthly cost report as his "bible." For operational control, however, he needed weekly costs and found it necessary to generate weekly estimates because decisions had to be made before monthly data were known. The controller at Engineering Software spoke of the difficulty of getting useful reports to their marketing divisions:

We send monthly product reports to the marketing divisions . . . orders, backlog, what's in backlog, shipments, margins on each product. These show trends and I think they are useful reports. But the problem is that they are not timely enough. We get them out by the 15th day of each month, when they really need them by the 4th or 5th day. The issue to people in the field is always timeliness. The challenge to us is to get information out in time that it can be useful to those who get it.

Simon (1954) noted these same problems and concerns with timeliness. He reported that where managers might have been able to use accounting exceptions, they had generally already learned of problems before reports were received.

Meeting the need for timely information means attending to two desires of operating managers. The first stems from their desire to be continuously aware of the status of operations and the possible need for action or redirection of effort because of unexpected events or changes. The second is their desire for accuracy, or confidence that they can act once information is received.

Accuracy

Trust in the accuracy of numbers is an obvious key element in the usefulness of information, yet many reports were cited during our interviews for deficiencies on this dimension.

Right now we get the raw data from phone calls to the plant, then we calculate the loads here. I don't think we'll see this report come out of the system any time soon because I'm not sure the people who would input the data appreciate the importance of their accuracy to us. It's nice to have a report, but if you can't be convinced it's 99 percent accurate, it's no good to you.

Sometimes accuracy or its lack was tied to implementation of new systems that had yet to be cleared of bugs. Too frequently, however, problems with the numbers seemed built into the system. At Belton Foods, the distribution manager trusted the general number of cases of finished goods in inventory, but not the specific breakdown. At Puraire, entire columns of data were dismissed because they had not been updated for six months. At other companies, multiple databases with inconsistent definitions or different measurement bases contributed to accuracy problems.

Relevance

Timeliness and accuracy contribute to the relevance of data. In addition, managers want information reported to them by certain categories with specific useful relationships delineated. The message that arbitrary cost allocations lead to dysfunctional decision making appears to have permeated the companies in our study, as we found only isolated problems with this much talked about taboo. Instead, most problems with accounting data relevance centered around the suboptimal categorization of data or the failure of the system to present desired relationships in reports.

Classification schemes that may be appropriate at some levels may not be appropriate from an operational standpoint. The manager of coke and iron production at Stanga Steel expressed frustration at his inability to use accounting reports to evaluate the blacksmith shop.

These cost reports are too detailed and formatted wrong. Look, here's the blacksmith shop costs, a piece in this category, a piece on this other page, a piece here, a piece there. I have to go all the way through this report adding pieces to get all the blacksmith shop costs. But even these numbers don't give me a vital piece of information I need, which is whether using our own blacksmith shop was preferable to using an external source.

Part of his frustration stems from his company's failure to redesign reports intended for financial reporting to better serve purposes of expenditures control. This particular company lags behind most others in its computerization of management information systems and is attempting to rectify the situation. However, problems of categorization and accumulation of information exist at companies that have sophisticated computerized systems. Failure to design a database so that useful relationships can be presented is a common problem that is difficult to rectify after the fact.

Corroboration, Redundancy, and Data Presentation

The way managers feel about the information they receive and use is sometimes a function of their confidence that the information is timely, accurate, and relevant. Corroborating information from a second source adds to the manager's perceived value of the information. Some redundancy is valued, and the consistency of different information adds to the confidence with which a manager uses information.

A plant manager may see relationships in information about employee absences, production line downtime, plant efficiency, and employee cafeteria revenues. A sales or marketing manager may see corroboration in the number of orders received, call reports, competitive prices, inventory levels, and economic news from national industry sources. The chief financial officer at Engineering Software told us:

I get information about production directly from them, but also from cost accounting. Much of the production data is not accounting data. There are other metrics like on-time delivery to customers, how many vendor schedule changes we have. There are a lot of different metrics we use to assure we have good inventory integrity. We're constantly reviewing that information.

The interrelationships observed in such information give every element greater value and let a manager act with greater confidence than when they are absent.

Another factor that adds to the usefulness of information for operations is the form in which the data are presented. Numerous studies have reaffirmed that data format does affect its use. For example, Edward Blocher, Robert Moffie, and Robert Zmud (1985) found in an experiment that simple tasks were done more accurately using colorful graphs, while complex tasks were more accurately accomplished with a tabular format of numerical data. Iris Vessey (1991) found that graphs allow people to grasp trends among numbers more quickly but less accurately than when they spent a few more seconds with tables. In our study, useful daily operations data generally did not lend themselves to colors or graphs because of the urgency of getting the data into the hands of the managers. Quite frequently, daily information was handwritten by workers on the floor using a standardized form to enter downtime, output, and so forth. Graphs and bar charts began to appear on monthly data and were cited frequently as more useful to managers because they could visually see the impact of numbers rather than have to add an interpretation step to their analyses.

An interesting example of the visual nature of data presentation exists at Scitron, where a measles board has replaced a computerized report. For each type of test instrument assembled, there is a diagram of the system on the wall at the workstation. As problems in materials are encountered, a pin is stuck to the diagram. Scitron has found this to be better for isolating problem components than the preexisting computer report. As the manager states:

What was wrong with the computer report was that it required a certain amount of computer literacy in order to be able to get an "Aha!" out of it. And the people that we need to get "Aha's!" from are the people operating that production process out there, and many of them aren't computer literate.

The value of absolute primary counts of factors such as units, downtime, workers, and scrap is enhanced by comparison to benchmarks or by manipulation with other variables into secondary counting measures. Actual output in units can be measured against expected or potential output. Unit output per machine or shift or worker provides a yield or measure of efficiency. A Maryland food plant manager looks at two key measures on arrival each morning: efficiency of the line measured by percentage of uptime and yield of ingredients measured as pounds produced divided by pounds of ingredients used.

Deli brisket is a big product for us and the yield on that beef is extremely important. It's $2.50 to $3 per pound, so if you've got a standard yield of 65 percent and I'm starting to see daily yields of 61 or 62, I know something's wrong . . . maybe something's happened to the slicing equipment, maybe we've lost control of the scaler on the line . . . it's something on a daily basis that tells me something's not right here.

The value of benchmarks, whether in variance format or expressed as yields, is dependent on many factors. Two of the most significant of these are the perceived reasonableness of the benchmark and experience level or gut feeling of the manager about the meaning of variations.

It is a well-established tenet in accounting literature that financial goals such as standard costs, budgeted expenditure levels, and budgeted revenue levels must be reasonably attainable and controllable in order to influence managerial actions properly (Simon, 1954; Kenneth Merchant, 1989, among others). However, this is also the case with simple counts and variances from counts. When the benchmark is flawed, or perceived to be biased, the manager compensates by establishing internal benchmarks based on personal experience. Regarding the Daily Blast Furnace report, the manager of coke and iron production quoted in Chapter 5 commented:

We're given these benchmarks that appear on all the charts. But this number doesn't mean anything now because we're in a different place. . . . The "expected" number is just a monthly average.

Sometimes a flawed benchmark becomes so ingrained that its value exists in the knowledge of how production output must differ from the standard each day or production period in order to meet the schedule. In one company, the plants estimate their future production levels in an annual budgeting process. After the budgeting process in which production schedules are initially set, top management notifies the plants of the extra production they must achieve in order to accomplish corporate goals.

I have a feel on a daily basis what our variance to budget ought to be. I look more at yields variance to budget than at actual numbers because I'm committed to a certain performance over the course of a year and over and above the budget. I know on a daily basis how that variance ought to be growing and if it's not growing, then I need to get into specifics and look at areas.

Why Accounting Fails to Satisfy Information Needs

Accounting only records and reports what has already happened. Between the moment of observation and the preparation and dissemination of a report, some amount of time elapses in even the most sophisticated computerized reporting systems. By the time observations made by operators, supervisors, or managers are accumulated into accounting reports, new events and activities are already under way. Even the best accounting is necessarily "old news" by some measures.

Managers see and feel an immediacy in their work. They have an innate need to take action on or to monitor what is happening now. Physical flows and current reports of events and activities coming from subordinates or associates are visible and available for managerial consideration, evaluation, and action, often before they have been observed by an accounting process. Observation and verbal reports confirm expectations or demand explanation and action, and managers are ready to get on with it. They prefer to be actors rather than analysts. While yesterday's events may be of interest, today's events are accompanied by a sense of urgency, action, and relevance. Only when data or information are confusing or contradictory does a manager consider waiting until a special study or accounting report arrives.

Aggregation and allocations, both of which are the basis of many accounting processes and accounting information, tend to obscure details that are important to managers. An injury to an employee disappears into the accumulated costs in a production report. A sales report from a field representative who has just met with a major customer is lost in the report on sales that will later be distributed by accounting. Allocations obscure cause-and-effect relationships between actions and events. Many management actions are nothing more than immediate reactions to small events, which are obscured by the process of measuring, aggregating, and reporting on activities.

None of these failings suggests that accounting is unnecessary and wasteful. Instead, they suggest that efforts to speed up accounting processes in hopes of meeting more of managers' information needs may be misdirected. Accounting processes and reports have roles to play in the management of every organization, but they must be seen as only a part of the much larger set of information managers want and use.

How Accounting Helps Managers

It is in the contemplation of what all the frenetic activity of day-to-day management adds up to that accounting reports and information contribute most to management. The blips and bleeps of day-to-day events accumulate and are averaged through time. In an accounting report, managers can view their tasks and their success or failure in a different way from that allowed by the day-to-day information they need to do their jobs. Many accounting reports give managers a sense of the business beyond their own job responsibilities or influence. Managers can evaluate the success of cross-functional coordination. Learning is fostered, and the mental model of the business that every manager creates and uses as a basis for analysis and actions is reinforced or modified. One general manager told us: "One of the things that I harp on around here is using the information to learn from. Don't make the same mistake twice."

A sales manager stressed his concern that some managers were poorly prepared to use accounting reports:

There's not enough understanding of accounting in general . . . it's probably a weakness of most managers. A good high-level manager has to be able to relate what his area is doing to a profit. If you can't, you can believe that sooner or later someone will bring that to your attention. Good senior managers take the time to educate themselves.

Accounting reports are important parts of the processes by which managers evaluate themselves and others evaluate their organizational performance. These evaluations typically follow managers' actions by days or weeks. There is seldom any urgency in getting reports used for evaluation into managers' hands. What is important is that a report contains information that permits a comparison of results with those expected over time periods long enough to average daily perturbations into a meaningful pattern.

The performance of managers is often evaluated in terms that match elements measured by accounting. Sales and marketing may be evaluated in terms of sales revenue or in terms of sales revenue compared with marketing and distribution expenses. Manufacturing or plant management may be evaluated in terms of the effectiveness with which costs have been controlled, or by a measure of operating efficiency. Business unit or product managers may be evaluated in terms of profitability, return on assets, or return on investment.

Managers told us that their own performance is frequently evaluated in terms of their effectiveness against these accounting measures. Goals and objectives are set through planning and negotiation. The measures of performance variables included in accounting reports then become a measure of their success. Because achieving what was expected can lead to rewards such as job satisfaction, pay raises, and future assignments, performance measures can be very important to managers. They regard them not only as necessary but as essential information for evaluating their own success. A general manager at Belton Foods described some of the measures against which he is evaluated (over 50 percent of which are associated with financial accounting earnings) in contrast to the measures he uses to operate daily:

What is most useful for following my bonus is specified target objectives data. This is proportioned at 25 percent volume; 40 percent operating earnings; 15 percent return on invested capital; and 20 percent specific operating objectives. But for running my operations, the most useful data are the package of plant efficiency statistics that I developed myself, which unfortunately will die when I'm transferred, as it's not a formal part of the system.

As managers review their success as reported in accounting reports, they are continuously at work, testing and perfecting their mental model of the relationship between activities and success as measured by the management accounting system. Remembering the events and activities that occurred during the period of time covered by an accounting report, and then seeing their success as reported by accounting, allow managers to associate events and activities with a level of organizational financial performance. Furthermore, in meetings where financial or accounting reports are reviewed and explained, the linkages between physical events and financial outcomes are reinforced. In this way, part of the accounting model is incorporated by managers into their own models. Managers learn to associate actions with organizational performance and success. All of this supports the conclusion that accounting information is very important, even though managers may not realize it or show it in their frenetic search for the information they need for day-to-day management.

Tailoring Reports to Managers' Training

Many of the managers we interviewed had training in accounting, while others told us they had never studied accounting or had had only minimal exposure to it in executive seminars. We were curious to try to learn if managers who had studied accounting would choose accounting reports as their most useful to a greater extent than

Exhibit 7-1 Most Useful Reports to Managers with Different
Accounting Knowledge (percentage of managers choosing)

Accounting Training or Experience	Accounting Degree CPA/CA/CMA	Business Degree or MBA	Some Study of Accounting in Executive Development Courses	No Accounting Education
Number of Managers*	15	31	13	12
Frequency of most useful report:				
Daily	7%	32%	46%	50%
Weekly	13	10	8	–
Monthly	73	45	31	50
Other	7	13	15	–
Content of most useful report:				
Unit data	27%	52%	69%	92%
Financial	73	45	15	8
No reports	–	3	15	–
Job function specific	13	48	54	75
General report	87	48	31	25
Size of report				
1–4 pages	47%	45%	46%	83%
> 4 pages	53	52	31	17

*Two interviews did not address this issue.

those managers who had not had this training. In other words, can managers be trained to use management accounting reports with more confidence and effectiveness? Exhibit 7-1 summarizes the characteristics of most useful reports of managers classified by their professed accounting training.

Several complications prevent us from making a strong claim that accounting training makes a difference. Job assignments consider training and, as we have shown in earlier chapters, different jobs require different kinds of information on a day-to-day or longer-term basis. Thus selection of a most useful report may have as much or more to do with a manager's job as it does with training in accounting. The small size of our samples prevents us from separating the effects of job and accounting training.

That said, the data we collected do appear to show systematic differences in the most useful reports named by managers with more background in accounting compared with those selected by managers with less such background. A greater proportion of reports named most useful by managers with more training in accounting cover longer reporting periods, include financial information, report on more than job function information, and are several pages in length. In contrast, those with less training in accounting appear more likely to prefer short reports containing unit data related to their job function. While we cannot eliminate the possibility of alternative explanations or causes for report selections by managers, these data suggest other interesting possibilities for ways in which the value of management accounting reports can be enhanced.

When reports are not or cannot be matched to the educational background and experience of managers, there is considerable risk that some of the value of reports to support learning will be lost. Reports that are not understood or are ignored do not add to the knowledge base that managers need to develop. Special care in report design may be one way to overcome this problem. Special efforts by management accountants to follow up on each report with meetings and explanations may be another. Our data suggest that problems in report usage may remain invisible as those who cannot make good use of reports simply ignore them, while those who do make good use assume others do as well.

Another possible response to these data would be to try to tailor management accounting reports to both the job function and the educational and experience background of a manager. This would add considerable complexity to the management accounting task.[1] Furthermore, job changes by managers would suggest frequent report changes. But two other possibilities exist. If managers could design their own reports out of a flexible database, their most useful reports could easily be matched to their job function, educational background, and cognitive skills and style. Computer and communication technologies offer potential in approaching such a solution, but only one of the companies we visited had systems that even begin to allow such flexibility. Alternatively, manager development programs could enhance the accounting education of managers who lack understanding of accounting concepts and reports. Whether this second alternative is really necessary or viable seems somewhat questionable, and we stop short of suggesting that it would enhance the value of information to managers.

The Fallacy of Information Overload

It has been alleged that under certain circumstances managers might get so much information that they would be overwhelmed and perhaps even unable to act because of what has been termed "information overload." We saw no evidence of this alleged phenomenon. None of the 73 managers with whom we talked told us that they felt overloaded with information. Instead, we heard descriptions of how managers use enormous quantities of data and information. Some managers told us they receive too many reports or that they receive reports that are too big to be useful. But that is a different issue from information overload, and there seems to be little risk that management accountants or other information providers can develop systems that will overwhelm the managers whom they are trying to serve.

The idea that information overload might exist for managers is probably rooted in one of three or four experiences or beliefs common to most people. Most of us have experienced one or two incidents where it seemed as if we knew so much about a subject that we found it difficult to choose a beginning point for action. The psychological panic that such an experience can evoke sometimes causes us to obscure or ignore our conflicting motives, or emotional attachment to a possible course of action different from the one we know we should or must take. Second, every human being has experienced asking for information on a subject and receiving so much information that it was impossible to find the relevant piece for the particular question we had in mind. Third, in their attempt to provide information to managers, accountants and other information providers sometimes supply source data, or data so detailed that the aggregation that would make it useful as managerial information must be done by the recipient at high cost in terms of time and effort. Finally, there is a body of literature based on psychological research that implies that human beings have a limited range of ability to focus on data or signals at any one point in time, and more information increases confidence in decisions without improving effectiveness.[2]

The managers whom we interviewed varied greatly in describing the amount of information that they seek and use for a particular task or activity in which they are regularly engaged. Some needed only a small amount of information. Others used more, assembling bits and pieces of data and information from different sources and arranging them so they could choose between the alternative courses of action open to them. But as we discussed their use of information, none said that sometimes they had so much information that they were unable to act or were rendered helpless in the face of a choice that had to be made.

Human beings are able to comprehend and process enormous amounts of information. Further, the ability to process information is part of the learning that takes place as people familiarize themselves with an activity or job. Michael Prietula and Herbert Simon (1989) have written about expertise in terms of a manager's ability to absorb and evaluate large quantities of information quickly because linked patterns are treated as a chunk of understanding and linked to other chunks. All of the managers with whom we spoke were experienced; hence it is not surprising that many have a highly developed ability to sort through enormous quantities of information and to focus on the elements that are critical to the decision or task at hand.

We conclude that for experienced managers, the notion of information overload has been exaggerated. The informational needs of managers are well within the abilities of human beings to receive, process, and use information. Perhaps novice managers can be overwhelmed, just as a new driver sometimes experiences panic in traffic, but few organizations would put a novice manager in the positions occupied by those we interviewed.

Some managers did tell us about another form of overload that has its roots in poor report design and distribution. They told us that they received too many reports or reports that were not useful because the information in them was too voluminous or was not arranged in an effective way. This is a different problem from overload. For this reason, we believe that if overload exists, it does not consist of managers receiving too much information, but rather receiving it in a form which makes the information impossible to find or too costly to use.

One form of paper report overload that managers showed us was large multipage, machine-generated reports. Computers and modern computer printers are capable of printing vast numbers of datapoints, observations, and measurements very quickly. Because summaries of information frequently elicit questions to the information provider, the information provider may simply decide to send the source data as well. The result of such a decision is much less helpful to a manager than the information provider may think. If the source data or unsummarized information are not in the form that allows a manager to find what he or she needs to know, they will leave much the same feeling as the implied notion of information overload. Recall how one Garrison's manager described his frustration at wanting to know the amount of product being sold by a grocery chain, but receiving data that listed the sales by individual store, requiring him to search through the entire report and add up the sales at that chain's stores to get the information he wanted. A marketing manager at Scitron said much the same thing:

rescheduled shipments, quantity variances, and inventory quantities. Associated with these is interest in inventory turnover, a secondary counting measure.

14. They are highly interested (as mentioned in #1) in changes to budget or forecast.

15. Surprisingly, they show more interest in profit margin on sales than any other group.

16. The remaining secondary measures of interest to this group involve costing of products, full cost and variable cost of products, and inventory value.

While Situation 1 was designed to elicit responses on information items considered important for everyday operations and operational control, Situation 2 was intended to lengthen the operating period and to introduce issues of longer-term performance measurement. We hypothesized that secondary measures and accounting and financial measures would be seen as more useful as the operating period was lengthened. Comparison of the rankings of selected information items in Tables 2 and 3 tends to support this hypothesis, especially in the rankings made by accountants and production managers.

Situation 2 (information items important at time of quarterly performance evaluation of managed division or department)—Table 3—differs from Situation 1.

For accountants . . .

17. The three budget-versus-actual measures remain at the top of the list for evaluation purposes.

18. The "what's been going on on an everyday basis?" measures largely disappear in this situation, several replaced by overall measures. New employees is replaced by total employees; delinquent accounts is replaced with receivables turnover (a secondary measure). Units produced and shipped disappear, as does cash payments.

19. Everyday overall measures such as prime rate, watch over special projects, and economic data disappear for evaluation purposes.

20. Replacing day-to-day watch over units made and shipped are more overall, secondary counting and financial measures such

as inventory turnover, cost of goods sold, and sales mix by product unit and product revenue.

21. Secondary financial measures such as return on assets (ROA) (this time by company in addition to by division), and profit margin on sales are still ranked quite highly.

For marketing managers . . .

22. Marketing measures for evaluation are more similar to their everyday operating measures than for accountants or production managers. They seem to evaluate using the same information used in operating, with emphasis on market shares, sales mixes, new customers, advertising expenditures, and so forth.

23. Some secondary financial measures increase in importance, notably profit margin by product and sales mix by product revenue.

24. Cost of goods sold and inventory turnover, which are secondary measures of product flow, appear for evaluation when they were not ranked highly for operations.

25. Finally, marketing managers show concerns with collecting sales, as the level of receivables enters the list at the bottom.

For production managers . . .

26. Information items selected for evaluation are characterized by more secondary measures, replacing the primary measures selected for operating management.

27. Everyday measures such as backlog, rejects, maintenance, orders taken, and so forth, either disappear or fall in importance.

28. The full cost of units produced becomes more important and the variable cost less important.

29. More complex variance measures such as materials usage variances, overhead variances, and capacity utilization increase in importance.

30. Several sales and profit measures gain in importance. Sales budgeted versus actual is ranked high for the first time, as is profit margin on sales and return on assets (ROA) by division.

Two other points are worthy of note. Eighteen of the twenty-six items added by respondents were primary counting measures. In addition, when items were weighted to reflect where they were ranked, there were no significant changes from the conclusions above, which are based solely on selection anywhere in the list of information items chosen.

Analysis of Information Item Choices by Item Classification

Because the survey questionnaire contained items representing (or respondents identified and selected) seventy-seven primary measures and forty-five secondary measures, which we also classified as sixty-eight counting measures and fifty-four financial measures, merely reporting total counts is potentially misleading. For this reason Table 4 also summarizes the average number of items selected by respondents in each classification, or per capita selections. The intention is to show how average selections of accountants and other respondents changed between Situation 1 and Situation 2. A t test was used to test whether the mean number of selections in the two situations and by accountants and others were different, and the results of these tests are also shown in Table 4.

The first section of Table 4 summarizes the choices of items that are primary measures compared to items that are secondary measures. For everyday operational control, there appears to be no difference between the average number of primary measures selected by accountants and nonaccountants, with each choosing approximately 4.3 items each. Nonaccountants chose more secondary measures on average than accountants (4.11 vs. 4.02) but the difference is small (this group also chose more items in total). Overall, more primary measures than secondary measures were chosen by each group (4.33 vs. 4.07).

Both groups selected many more secondary measures for evaluation than for everyday operational control. Nonaccountants selected more primary measures than accountants for evaluation (3.44 vs. 2.92) and more secondary ones as well (5.28 vs. 4.70).

The second section of Table 4 summarizes the choices classified as counting versus financial items. Accountants selected more financial measures than counting measures for both control and evaluation, with the difference more significant in the latter case (4.38 vs. 3.24). Nonaccountants chose more counting measures than financial measures for operations (4.77 vs. 3.68) and more financial measures than counting measures for evaluation (4.64 vs. 4.04).

Table 4 Information Item Choices by Classification

	ALL	Per Capita	Accounts	Per Capita	Others	Per Capita
I. PRIMARY (77 items)						
Vacation	532	[4.33	215	[4.30	3.17	[4.34
Evaluation	397	3.23]	146	2.92]	251	3.44]*
SECONDARY (45 items)						
Vacation	501	[4.07	201	[4.02]#	300	[4.11
Evaluation	618	5.02]	235	4.70	3.83	5.28]**
II. COUNTING (68 items)						
Vacation	543	[4.41	195	[3.90]#	348	[4.77]*
Evaluation	456	3.72]	162	3.24	296	4.04]*
FINANCIAL (54 items)						
Vacation	490	[3.98	221	4.42	269	3.68
Evaluation	558	4.51]	219	4.38	339	4.64

III. PRIMARY/COUNT						
(59 items)						
Vacation	431	[3.50]	170	[3.54]	261	[3.58]*
Evaluation	338	[2.75]	118	[2.36]	220	[3.01]*
PRIMARY/FINANCIAL						
(18 items)						
Vacation	86	[.70]	45	[.90]	41	.56*
Evaluation	59	[.48]	25	[.50]	38	.52
SECOND/COUNT						
(9 items)						
Vacation	112	.91	20	[.40]	92	1.26*
Evaluation	134	1.09	45	[.90]	89	1.22**
SECOND/FINANCIAL						
(36 items)						
Vacation	404	[3.29]#	181	3.62	233	[3.19]*
Evaluation	484	[4.00]	193	3.86	291	[3.99]
IV. TOTALS						
Vacation	1,033	8.40 per capita				
Evaluation	1,015	8.25 per capita				

[ ] Difference between vacation and evaluation choices is significant at .05 level.
[ ]# Difference between vacation and evaluation choices is significant at .10 level.
* Difference between choices of accountants and others is significant at .05 level.
** Difference between choices of accountants and others is significant at .10 level.

The third section of Table 4 reports per capita selection by classification cells. The primary/counting cell was the largest combined category, with 59 items chosen a total of 769 times. Both groups selected about the same per capita for vacation, but nonaccountants listed more primary/counting items to be used for evaluation. The secondary/financial cell was the second largest combined category, with 36 items chosen a total of 888 times. Accountants chose more secondary/financial information items than nonaccountants for operational control but about the same for evaluation. The other two cells are too small to be meaningful.

Conclusions, Implications, and Further Research

The limited nature of the questionnaire survey limits any attempt at this time to prescribe from our findings. As usual, a call for further research is both necessary and appropriate. However, exploratory results lead to some tentative conclusions about the information managers want and the design or adaptation of management information systems. Managers use many kinds of data and information. Accounting information, especially secondary measures, may be much less important to managers than some previous accounting research may have assumed. Designers of technology-supported executive information systems, decision support systems, and management information systems may be well advised to include primary accounting measures and other information, as well as secondary accounting measures, to the fullest extent possible until information-use patterns by managers are better understood.

The preliminary evidence that accountants and financial managers may prefer more secondary and financial measures may be the result of one or both of two factors. First, their tasks and job characteristics may make such information more important to them. Second, training and experience may make them more comfortable with the content, meaning, and utility of the somewhat more complex measurements and information. (We reject a third explanation for this preference—that accountants do not understand operations and therefore must resort to accounting reports for obfuscation.) If training and experience should prove to be the dominant reasons why accountants and financial managers use more complex accounting measurements, perhaps special training can help other managers learn to use these data more comfortably and effectively.

In many respects the variety of responses to the questionnaire in this study are consistent with the findings of Kotter (1982) about what general managers do, how managers think (Isenberg 1984, 1985a, and 1985b), and with the idea that managers used a form of decision making that approaches mixed scanning (Etzioni, 1967, 1986). They are also consistent with the conclusion that effective executive information systems use multiple and rapidly generated databases, many of which are oriented to providing managers with information to generate questions (Turban and Schaeffer, 1987; McLeod and Jones, 1986).

The large role that counting and primary measures may play in the use of information by managers also suggests that effective systems will concentrate on providing those measures in the most accurate and timely way possible. They may be essential inputs to the "cognitive constructs" that describe a person's understanding of a particular segment of the managerial world. Rockart and DeLong (1988) in particular have written at length on how executive support systems with greater access to data from multiple sources presented in meaningful formats seem to enhance the "mental models" of executives they studied.

More research into several of the issues raised from this survey is clearly warranted. But, one conclusion seems obvious and beyond question. Managers use an incredible variety of information collected from diverse sources, and accounting reports and analyses are only a part of that information, and perhaps a small part at that. This has important implications that should not be overlooked by accountants and others involved in the design of new executive and management support systems.

About the Authors

SHARON McKINNON is an Associate Professor of Business Administration at Northeastern University and serves as group coordinator of the accounting group. A graduate of the University of North Carolina, McKinnon also earned an MPA and a Ph.D. from Georgia State University. She has taught the Financial Accounting module of the Executive MBA program at Northeastern for the past nine years. She is co-author (with Thomas Edmonds) of *Financial Accounting: An Elements Approach* and *Accounting Principles* and author of *The Seventh Directive: Consolidated Accounts in Europe.* She has also published extensively in such periodicals as *Financial Analysts Journal, Journal of Business, Finance, and Accounting,* and *Management Accounting,* among others.

WILLIAM J. BRUNS, JR., is a graduate of the University of Redlands, Harvard (MBA), and the University of California at Berkeley (Ph.D.). He taught at Yale University and the University of Washington before joining the faculty of the Harvard Business School—where he teaches "Financial Reporting and Management Accounting." Professor Bruns has had extensive experience in executive education programs and consulting. He is co-editor (with Robert S. Kaplan) of *Accounting and Management: Field Studies Perspectives* and (with Don T. DeCoster) *Accounting and Its Behavioral Implications.* He is co-author (with M. Edgar Barrett) of *Case Problems in Management Accounting* and (with Richard F. Vancil) *A Primer on Replacement Cost Accounting,* and author of *Introduction to Accounting: Economic Measurement for Decisions.*

Index

Company names in italics are fictitious names of those researched for this project.